Animals of the Night

BULL SHARKS AFTER DARK

Heather M. Moore Niver

Enslow Publishing
101 W. 23rd Street
Suite 240
New York, NY 10011
USA

enslow.com

Words to Know

electroreception—The ability of an animal to sense electrical waves or vibrations in the water.

endangered—Threatened or in danger.

gland—An organ that makes and releases substances into the body or gets rid of substances.

habitat—The place in which an animal lives.

migrate—To move from one area or habitat to another.

nocturnal—Mostly active at night.

pectoral fins—The fins just on either side of a fish's head.

predators—Animals that kill and eat other animals to stay alive.

prey—An animal hunted by another animal for food.

requiem sharks—Sharks that live in warm seas, sometimes live in freshwater, and give birth to live babies.

Contents

Underwater Hunt

In the dark murky waters near the shore, all seems still. The sun has not yet risen for the day. But the bull shark swims slowly in the shadows. Its dark skin blends in so it can hardly be seen. The hungry bull shark senses a meal swimming ahead. It noses forward and butts the fish with its wide nose. Deciding that this fish is a worthy meal, it butts again—much harder this time. And with great speed, it attacks with big sharp teeth and rips into a satisfying fish breakfast.

FUN FACT!

Bull sharks are not picky eaters. They will sometimes eat animals much larger than they are. They have been known to eat a hippopotamus and cows.

Bull sharks sometimes head-butt an animal before deciding if it will make a good meal.

Behold, the Bull Shark

Bull sharks have a short, rounded nose. They also have small eyes. This may be because they don't use their eyesight as much as other senses. Compared to other sharks, they are medium-sized. They are between 7 and 11.5 feet (2.1 to 3.4 meters) long. Bull sharks weigh between 200 and 500 pounds (90 to 230 kilograms). Their bodies are thick and wide. In fact, their bodies are wider than they are long. Their **pectoral fins** are long. Most bull sharks have gray backs and white bellies. Their fins are dark on the ends, especially when they are young.

FUN FACT!

The bull shark's coloring helps it blend in. Dark coloring from the top helps it look like part of the water. When viewed from below, white bellies look like the sky.

The bull shark can swim along unnoticed

A Rough Bunch

Bull sharks are part of one of the largest groups of sharks called **requiem sharks**, or carcharhinid. Requiem sharks are a rough bunch. Many of the most aggressive sharks belong to this species, or kind, of shark. Some examples include tiger sharks, Caribbean reef sharks, blacktip sharks, and blue sharks.

Requiem sharks tend to be great swimmers. They have strong bodies and long fins.

Many requiem sharks like to be social. They hang out together and sometimes hunt. The bull shark and oceanic whitetips like life alone. Bull sharks will be more social when it's time to have babies.

FUN FACT!

The bull shark goes by many names, including cub shark, ground shark, Ganges shark, Zambezi shark, shovelnose, freshwater whaler, swan river whaler, or slipway grey.

Bull sharks are among the requiem sharks that like to swim alone.

Saltwater Magic Trick

Bull sharks live all over the world. They are not picky about what kind of water they are swimming in. Most of the time, bull sharks like to live in shallow waters along coasts. They are usually found swimming in the salt waters of the oceans. Bull sharks don't mind swimming up fresh water rivers, though. In Nicaragua they sometimes leap up river rapids.

But bull sharks need salt water to survive. If they are in freshwater for a long time, their bodies adapt. The kidneys and special **glands** in their tails help them keep the salt they need in their bodies.

Bull sharks have been seen in rivers, like this one in Costa Rica. They have also been found thousands of miles up the Amazon River.

Bull sharks can live in salt water or freshwater because their bodies have what some call "super kidneys." They can measure how much salt is in their blood and adjust to keep the shark healthy. This process is called osmoregulation. Sometimes they urinate in the water to get rid of salt in their bodies. Other times they get rid of salt through their gills. Usually their bodies adjust for salt gradually. This makes sure their kidneys don't work too hard, too.

FUN FACT!

Osmoregulation helps the bull shark make sure its body has enough salt. It also helps adjust so that it does not have too much.

Bull sharks can get rid of salt through their gills.

Dangerous!

Bull sharks are considered one of the most dangerous sharks in the world. This is partially because they like to live and hunt near shorelines. Here they are in contact with humans. Humans are not really on their to-hunt list, but they may attack humans by mistake or nibble out of curiosity. (A nibble to a shark is a serious injury to a human, though!)

Generally, bull sharks will eat anything they see. This might mean fish, dolphins, sea turtles, and other sharks. Sometimes they will even eat birds. Bull sharks are strong, aggressive hunters.

FUN FACT!

Bull shark attacks on humans are not common at all, but the bull shark is nicknamed the "pit bull of the sea."

quickly get up to 11 miles (18 kilometers) per hour. Bull sharks hunt by themselves. They swim slowly along the bottom of the water. Bull sharks have a great sense of smell, so they can sniff out their next meal. Their small eyes can adapt to changes easily. If there is sudden darkness or bright light, their eyes quickly adjust. Their eyes also have a special layer that protects them from being damaged.

Bull sharks swim slowly along the bottom of the water but put on a great burst of speed to attack.

My, What Sharp Teeth You Have!

A **predator** like a bull shark has to have great teeth for hunting. Bull sharks have different types of teeth on their upper and lower jaws. The top teeth are wide and triangle-shaped with edges like saws. The bottom teeth are narrow and triangle-shaped. They are also saw-like, but they have a finer sharpness than those on top. The rough edges are great for biting and tearing **prey**. Their teeth are replaced all throughout their life.

FUN FACT!

Bull sharks have the strongest bite of all the sharks.

The rough, saw-like edges of a bull shark's teeth are sharp and tear into their prey.

Bump and Bite

Bull sharks have a special way of hunting. The bull shark's wide nose helps it get its next dinner. The bull shark sometimes uses it to head-butt their prey. This slows the prey down or stuns them so the bull shark can get a good bite. They may use this method to make sure their prey is something they want to eat. Bull sharks often hunt in dark, cloudy water, so they can't always see very well. This way of hunting allows them to get close and check on their next meal without being noticed.

FUN FACT!

Bull sharks also have
a great sense of smell,
which helps on
the hunt.

The bull shark uses its wide nose to check out prey to see if it seems like a tasty treat.

Hey, Baby!

Bull sharks and other requiem sharks give birth to live babies. Before they are born, the babies grow inside the mother. The mother carries the babies for almost a year before giving birth. Babies are usually born in spring or summer, but in some areas of they world it can be any time of the year. Mother sharks give birth to up to 13 babies at a time. When they are born, the babies are about 28 inches (about 70 centimeters) long.

FUN FACT!

A group of sharks is
called a school or
a shoal.

Just like this lemon shark, bull sharks give birth to live young.

Mother bull sharks don't give birth to their babies just anywhere. Pregnant bull sharks **migrate** to areas where the tide meets the mouth of a river, or estuary. They move to raise their young in the safety of freshwater until it starts to get too cold for the babies. Then they move back to warmer waters.

Some bull sharks have been known to move from cooler area to warmer spots. Along the East coast, they have sometimes moved north in the summer as those waters get warm. They move south again as it cools off.

This pregnant bull shark will give birth and raise her young in an estuary.

Bull sharks have another handy skill that helps them migrate and hunt. Many sharks, including bull sharks, have what some scientists call a "seventh sense" called **electroreception**. Besides a great sense of smell, this sense helps them detect vibrations in the water. Near their noses are tiny holes, or pores. Connected to these pores are jelly-filled bulbs, which also connect to the shark's nerves. These pores sense other sharks and prey as they move and send out electrical pulses. Electroreception also works as a compass to help sharks when they migrate.

FUN FACT!

Many sharks have thousands of pores that sense vibrations in the water.

The pores used in electroreception are called ampullae of Lorenzini.

Save Our Sharks

Bull sharks are not on the official danger list for being **endangered**. But official counts of bull sharks suggest that they are "near threatened." Bull sharks don't have many enemies, but they have one threatening one: humans. Fishermen who are fishing for other fish accidentally catch bull sharks in their fishing nets. When they are caught, though, bull sharks are sold for their skin (leather), liver (oil), and fins (soup). They are also in danger of pollution and changes to their **habitats** by humans.

Bull sharks are sometimes targeted by fishermen who want their impressive jaws.

Stay Safe Around Bull Sharks

Bull sharks swim and hunt near shores and others places where there are lots of humans. Shark attacks are not common, but it's important to know how to be safe when swimming in areas where there might be bull sharks.

- 🌙 Bull sharks are **nocturnal**. They don't swim at night or early in morning.
- 🌙 Get out of the water if you see fish jumping out of the water; something is probably chasing them.
- 🌙 Don't swim in cloudy water where bull sharks like to hunt. Sometimes waters are cloudy after a storm. Wait until they clear before heading in.
- 🌙 Don't splash around. The shark might think you are prey, especially in cloudy water where it can't see.
- 🌙 If you are attacked, hit the shark on the nose. If that doesn't work, scratch at its eyes and gills.

Learn More

Books

Hopper, Whitney. *In Search of Bull Sharks*. New York: Powerkids Press, 2016.

Kennington, Tammy. *Bull Sharks*. Ann Arbor, MI: Cherry Lake Publishing, 2014.

Nagelhout, Ryan. *Diving With Sharks*. New York: Gareth Stevens, 2014.

Niver, Heather Moore. *20 Fun Facts About Sharks*. New York: Gareth Stevens, 2012.

Websites

National Geographic: Bull Shark

animals.nationalgeographic.com/animals/fish/bull-shark/
Check out bull shark photos, facts, maps, and more!

National Wildlife Federation: Bull Shark

www.nwf.org/Wildlife/Wildlife-Library/Amphibians-Reptiles-and-Fish/Bull-Shark.aspx
Fun facts and photos help readers learn more about bull sharks.

BioExpedition: Bull Shark

www.bioexpedition.com/bull-shark/
This website features loads of photos and facts about bull sharks.

Index

Published in 2017 by Enslow Publishing, LLC.
101 W. 23rd Street, Suite 240, New York, NY 10011

Library of Congress Cataloging-in-Publication Data
Names: Niver, Heather Moore, author.
Title: Bull sharks after dark / Heather M. Moore Niver.
Description: New York, NY, USA : Enslow Publishing, 2017. | Series: Animals of the night | Includes bibliographical references and index.
Identifiers: LCCN 2016001564| ISBN 9780766077126 (library bound) | ISBN 9780766077447 (pbk.) | ISBN 9780766076891 (6-pack)
Subjects: LCSH: Bull shark—Juvenile literature. | Nocturnal animals—Juvenile literature.
Classification: LCC QL638.95.C3 N58 2016 | DDC 597.3/4—dc23
LC record available at http://lccn.loc.gov/2016001564

Printed in the United States of America